Emerson

Emerson

Selections From *Self-Reliance*,

Friendship, *Compensation*,

and Other Great Writings

of Ralph Waldo Emerson

Selected by

Stanley Hendricks

HALLMARK EDITIONS

Contents

Emerson's Greatness

Matthew Arnold,
the renowned 19th-century English poet and
critic, is best known for his poem Dover Beach.
He lectured on Ralph Waldo Emerson
at Boston after the New England writer
and lecturer's death.
These paragraphs of tribute
come from that lecture:

We have not in Emerson a great poet, a great writer, a great philosophy-maker. His relation to us is not that of one of those personages; yet it is a relation of, I think, even superior importance. His relation to us is more like that of the Roman Emperor Marcus Aurelius. Marcus Aurelius is not a great writer, a great philosophy-maker; he is the friend and the aider of those who would live in the spirit. Emerson is the same. He is the friend and aider of those who would live in the spirit.

All the points in thinking which are necessary for this purpose he takes; but he does not combine them into a system, or present them as a regular philosophy. Combined in a system by a man with the requisite talent for this kind of thing, they would be less useful than as Emerson gives them to us; and the man with the talent so to systematise them would be less impressive than Emerson. They do very well as they now stand — like 'boulders,' as he says — in 'paragraphs incompressible, each sentence an infinitely repellent particle.' In such sentences his main points recur again and again, and become fixed in the memory. . . .

As Wordsworth's poetry is, in my judgment, the most important work done in verse, in our language, during the [19th] century, so Emerson's *Essays* are, I think, the most important work done in prose. . . .

By his conviction that in the life of the spirit is happiness, and by his hope that this life of the spirit will come more and more to be sanely understood, and to prevail, and to work for happiness—by this conviction and hope Emerson was great, and he will surely prove in the end to have been right in them. . . .

You cannot prize him too much, nor heed him too diligently. He has lessons for both the [English and American] branches of our race. . . . To us he shows for guidance his lucid freedom, his cheerfulness and hope; to you his dignity, delicacy, serenity, elevation.

Emerson

On Nature and the Natural Man

Ralph Waldo Emerson believed in a universe
where all things are connected.
"Life wears to me a visionary face," he says here.
He means that life can be read like the pages
of a book, that we can discover ourselves
in the world around us and the world around us
in ourselves. It is a deeply democratic vision.

You must treat the days respectfully, you must be a day yourself, and not interrogate it like a college professor. The world is enigmatical—everything said, and everything known or done—and must not be taken literally, but genially. We must be at the top of our condition to understand anything rightly. You must hear the bird's song without attempting to render it into nouns and verbs. Cannot we be a little abstemious and obedient? Cannot we let the morning be?

We are natural believers. Truth, or the connection between cause and effect, alone interests us. We are persuaded that a thread runs through all things: all words are strung on it, as beads; and

men, and events, and life, come to us only because of that thread: they pass and repass only
that we may know the direction and continuity
of that line. A book or statement which goes to
show that there is no line, but random and chaos,
a calamity out of nothing, a prosperity and no
account of it, a hero born from a fool, a fool from
a hero—dispirits us. Seen or unseen, we believe
the tie exists. Talent makes counterfeit ties;
genius finds the real ones.

Life wears to me a visionary face. Hardest
roughest action is visionary also. It is but a choice
between soft and turbulent dreams. People dis-
parage knowing and the intellectual life, and
urge doing. I am very content with knowing, if
only I could know. That is an august entertain-
ment, and would suffice me a great while. To
know a little would be worth the expense of this
world. I hear always the law of Adrastia, "that
every soul which had acquired any truth, should
be safe from harm until another period."

To speak truly, few adult persons can see nature.
Most persons do not see the sun. At least they
have a very superficial seeing. The sun illumi-
nates only the eye of the man, but shines into the
eye and the heart of the child. The lover of nature

is he whose inward and outward senses are still truly adjusted to each other; who has retained the spirit of infancy even into the era of manhood. His intercourse with heaven and earth becomes part of his daily food. In the presence of nature a wild delight runs through the man, in spite of real sorrows. Nature says—he is my creature, and maugre all his impertinent griefs, he shall be glad with me.

Not the sun or the summer alone, but every hour and season yields its tribute of delight; for every hour and change corresponds to and authorizes a different state of the mind, from breathless noon to grimmest midnight. Nature is a setting that fits equally well a comic or a mourning piece. In good health, the air is a cordial of incredible virtue. Crossing a bare common, in snow puddles, at twilight, under a clouded sky, without having in my thoughts any occurance of special good fortune, I have enjoyed a perfect exhilaration. I am glad to the brink of fear. In the woods, too, a man casts off his years, as the snake his slough, and at what period soever of life is always a child.

In the woods is perpetual youth. Within these plantations of God, a decorum and sanctity reign, a perennial festival is dressed, and the guest sees not how he should tire of them in a thousand years. In the woods we return to reason and faith. There I feel that nothing can befall me in life—no disgrace, no calamity (leaving me my eyes), which nature cannot repair. Standing on the bare ground—my head bathed by the blithe air, and uplifted into infinite space—all mean egotism vanishes. I become a transparent eyeball; I am nothing; I see all; the currents of the Universal Being circulate through me; I am part or parcel of God.

The terrible aristocracy that is in Nature. Real people dwelling with the real, face to face, undaunted: then, far down, people of taste, people dwelling in a relation, or rumor, or influence of good and fair, entertained by it, superficially touched, yet charmed by these shadows—and, far below these, gross and thoughtless, the animal man, billows of chaos, down to the dancing and menial organizations.

We all give way to superstitions. The house in which we were born is not quite mere timber and stone; is still haunted by parents and progenitors. The creeds into which we were initiated in childhood and youth no longer hold their old place in the minds of thoughtful men, but they are not nothing to us, and we hate to have them treated with contempt. There is so much that we do not know, that we give to these suggestions the benefit of the doubt.

We are always coming up with the emphatic facts of history in our private experience and verifying them here. All history becomes subjective; in other words there is properly no history, only biography. Every mind must know the whole lesson for itself—must go over the whole ground. What it does not see, what it does not live, it will not know. . . . The better for him.

In dreams we are true poets; we create the persons of the drama; we give them appropriate figures, faces, costume; they are perfect in their organs, attitude, manners: moreover they speak after their own characters, not ours—they speak to us, and we listen with surprise to what they say. Indeed, I doubt if the best poet has yet written any five-act play that can compare in thoroughness of invention with this unwritten play in fifty acts, composed by the dullest snorer on the floor of the watch-house.

We learn nothing rightly until we learn the symbolical character of life. Day creeps after day, each full of facts, dull, strange, despised things,

that we cannot enough despise—call heavy, pro-
saic and desert. The time we seek to kill: the at-
tention it is elegant to divert from things around
us. And presently the aroused intellect finds
gold and gems in one of these scorned facts—
then finds that the day of facts is a rock of dia-
monds; that a fact is an Epiphany of God.

Proverbs, like the sacred books of each nation,
are the sanctuary of the intuitions. That which
the droning world, chained to appearances, will
not allow the realist to say in his own words, it
will suffer him to say in proverbs without con-
tradiction. And this law of laws, which the pul-
pit, the senate and the college deny, is hourly
preached in all markets and workshops by flights
of proverbs, whose teaching is as true and as
omnipresent as that of birds and flies.

. . . The simple perception of natural forms is a
delight. The influence of the forms and actions in
nature is so needful to man that, in its lowest
functions, it seems to lie on the confines of commodity and beauty. To the body and mind which
have been cramped by noxious work or company,
nature is medicinal and restores their tone. The
tradesman, the attorney comes out of the din and
craft of the street and sees the sky and the woods,

and is a man again. In their eternal calm, he finds himself. The health of the eye seems to demand a horizon. We are never tired, so long as we can see far enough.

The inhabitants of cities suppose that the country landscape is pleasant only half the year. I please myself with the graces of the winter scenery, and believe that we are as much touched by it as by the genial influences of summer. To the attentive eye, each moment of the year has its own beauty, and in the same field, it beholds, every hour, a picture which was never seen before and which shall never be seen again.

The first care of a man settling in the country should be to open the face of the earth to himself by a little knowledge of Nature, or a great deal, if he can; of birds, plants, rocks, astronomy; in short, the art of taking a walk. This will draw the sting out of frost, dreariness out of November and March, and the drowsiness out of August.

By his machines man can dive and remain under water like a shark; can fly like a hawk in the air; can see atoms like a gnat; can see the system of the universe like Uriel, the angel of the sun; can carry whatever loads a ton of coal can lift; can knock down cities with his fist of gunpowder; can recover the history of his race by the medals which the deluge, and every creature, civil or savage or brute, has involuntarily dropped of its existence; and divine the future possibility of the planet and its inhabitants by his perception of laws of Nature. Ah! what a plastic little creature he is! so shifty, so adaptive! his body a chest of tools, and he making himself comfortable in every climate, in every condition.

Nature is a tropical swamp in sunshine, on whose purlieus we hear the song of summer birds, and see prismatic dewdrops—but her interiors are terrific, full of hydras and crocodiles.

There is a crack in everything God has made. It would seem there is always this vindictive circumstance stealing in at unawares even into the wild poesy in which the human fancy attempted to make bold holiday and to shake itself free of the old laws—this back-stroke, this kick of the gun, certifying that the law is fatal; that in nature nothing can be given, all things are sold.

Men are born to write. The gardener saves every slip and seed and peach-stone; his vocation is to be a planter of plants. Not less does the writer attend his affair. Whatever he beholds or experiences, comes to him as a model and sits for its picture. He counts it all nonsense that they say, that some things are undescribable. He believes that all that can be thought can be written, first or last; and he would report the Holy Ghost, or attempt it.

. . . When the mind opens and reveals the laws which traverse the universe and make things what they are, then shrinks the great world at once into a mere illustration and fable of this mind. What am I? and What is? asks the human spirit with a curiosity new-kindled, but never to be quenched. Behold these outrunning laws, which our imperfect apprehension can see tend this way and that, but not come full circle. Behold these infinite relations, so like, so unlike; many, yet one. I would study, I would know, I would admire forever. These works of thought have been entertainments of the human spirit in all ages.

It is curious to see how a creature so feeble and vulnerable as a man, who, unarmed, is no match for the wild beasts, tiger, or crocodile, none for the frost, none for the sea, none for fog or a damp air, or the feeble fork of a poor worm—each of a thousand petty accidents puts him to death every day—is yet able to subdue to his will these terrific forces, and more than these. His whole frame is responsive to the world, part for part, every sense, every pore to a new element, so that he seems to have as many talents as there are qualities in Nature. No force but is his force. He does not possess them, he is a pipe through which their currents flow. If a straw be held still in the direction of the ocean-current, the sea will pour through it as through Gibraltar. If he should measure strength with them, if he should fight the sea and the whirlwind with his ship, he would snap his spars, tear his sails, and swamp his bark; but by cunningly dividing the force, tapping the tempest for a little side-wind, he uses the monsters, and they carry him where he would go.

Dream delivers us to dream, and there is no end to illusion. Life is a train of moods like a string of beads, and as we pass through them they prove to be many-colored lenses which paint the world their own hue, and each shows only what lies in its focus. From the mountain you see the mountain. We animate what we can, and we see only what we animate. Nature and books belong to the eyes that see them. It depends on the mood of the man whether he shall see the sunset or the fine poem. There are always sunsets, and there is always genius; but only a few hours so serene that we can relish nature or criticism. The more or less depends on structures or temperament. Temperament is the iron wire on which the beads are strung.

. . . Nature is no sentimentalist—does not cosset or pamper us. We must see that the world is rough and surly, and will not mind drowning a man or a woman, but swallows your ship like a grain of dust. The cold, inconsiderate of persons, tingles your blood, benumbs your feet, freezes a man like an apple. The diseases, the elements, fortune, gravity, lightning, respect no persons. The way of Providence is a little rude. The habit of snake and spider, the snap of the tiger and other leapers and bloody jumpers, the crackle of the bones of his prey in the coil of the anaconda —these are in the system, and our habits are like theirs. You have just dined, and however scrupulously the slaughter-house is concealed in the graceful distance of miles, there is complicity, expensive races—race living at the expense of race. . . .

Providence has a wild, rough, incalculable road to its end, and it is of no use to try to whitewash its huge, mixed instrumentalities, or to dress up that terrific benefactor in a clean shirt and white neckcloth of a student in divinity.

Will you say, the disasters which threaten mankind are exceptional, and one need not lay his account for cataclysms every day? Aye, but what happens once may happen again, and so long as these strokes are not to be parried by us they must be feared.

But these shocks and ruins are less destructive to us than the stealthy power of other laws which act on us daily. An expense of ends to means is fate—organization tyrannizing over character. The menagerie, or forms and powers of the spine, is a book of fate; the bill of the bird, the skull of the snake, determines tyrannically its limits. So is the scale of races, of temperaments; so is sex; so is climate; so is the reaction of talents imprisoning the vital power in certain directions. Every spirit makes its house; but afterwards the house confines the spirit.

Language is fossil poetry. As the limestone of the continent consists of infinite masses of the shells of animalcules, so language is made up of images or tropes, which now, in their secondary use, have long ceased to remind us of their poetic origin.

On Character and Self-Reliance

*If nature is visionary and the world a place
of interconnected events, then man must
make himself. This is the essence of Emerson's
view of human character—that it must be
shaped by the owner to fit his own frame.
Thoreau's hesitant "Beware of all enterprises
that require new clothes" becomes Emerson's
assertive "I do not see how any man can
afford, for the sake of his nerves and his nap,
to spare any action in which he can partake."*

There is no privacy that cannot be penetrated.
No secret can be kept in the civilized world. Society is a masked ball, where everyone hides his
real character, and reveals it by hiding. If a man
wishes to conceal anything he carries, those
whom he meets know that he conceals somewhat,
and usually know what he conceals. Is it other-
wise if there be some belief or some purpose he
would bury in his breast? 'Tis as hard to hide as
fire. He is a strong man who can hold down his
opinion. A man cannot utter two or three sentences without disclosing to intelligent ears pre-

cisely where he stands in life and thought, name-
ly, whether in the kingdom of the senses and the
understanding, or in that of ideas and imagination, in the realm of intuitions and duty. People
seem not to see that their opinion of the world is
also a confession of character.

Life is our dictionary. Years are well spent in
country labors; in town; in the insight into
trades and manufactures; in frank intercourse
with many men and women; in science; in art;
to the one end of mastering in all their facts a
language by which to illustrate and embody our
perceptions. I learn immediately from any
speaker how much he has already lived, through
the poverty or the splendor of his speech. Life
lies behind us as the quarry from whence we get
tiles and copestones for the masonry of today.
This is the way to learn grammar. Colleges and
books only copy the language which the field and
the workyard made.

What opium is instilled into all disaster! It shows
formidable as we approach it, but there is at last
no rough rasping friction, but the most slippery
sliding surfaces; we fall soft on a thought. . . .
There are moods in which we court suffering, in
the hope that here at least we shall find reality,

sharp peaks and edges of truth. But it turns out to be scene-painting and counterfeit. The only thing grief has taught me is to know how shallow it is.

God offers to every mind its choice between truth and repose. Take which you please—you can never have both. Between these, as a pendulum, man oscillates. He in whom the love of repose predominates will accept the first creed, the first philosophy, the first political party he meets— most likely his father's. He gets rest, commodity and reputation; but he shuts the door of truth. He in whom the love of truth predominates will keep himself aloof from all moorings, and afloat. He will abstain from dogmatism, and recognize all the opposite negations between which, as walls, his being is swung. He submits to the inconvenience of suspense and imperfect opinion....

No sane man at last distrusts himself. His existence is a perfect answer to all sentimental cavils. If he is, he is wanted, and has the precise properties that are required. That we are here, is proof we ought to be here.

Men are in all ways better than they seem. They like flattery for the moment, but they know the truth for their own. It is a foolish cowardice which keeps us from trusting them and speaking to them rude truth. They resent your honesty for an instant, they will thank you for it always. What is it we heartily wish of each other? Is it to be pleased and flattered? No, but to be convicted and exposed, to be shamed out of our nonsense of all kinds, and made men of, instead of ghosts and phantoms. We are weary of gliding ghost-like through the world, which is itself so slight and unreal. We crave a sense of reality, though it comes in strokes of pain.

To believe your own thought, to believe that what is true for you in your private heart is true for all men—that is genius. Speak your latent conviction, and it shall be the universal sense; for the inmost in due time becomes the outmost, and our first thought is rendered back to us by the trumpets of the Last Judgment. Familiar as the voice of the mind is to each, the highest merit we ascribe to Moses, Plato and Milton is that they set at naught books and traditions, and spoke not what men, but what *they* thought.

A man should learn to detect and watch that gleam of light which flashes across his mind from within, more than the lustre of the firmament of bards and sages. Yet he dismisses without notice his thought, because it is his. In every work of genius we recognize our own rejected thoughts; they come back to us with a certain alienated majesty. They teach us to abide by our spontaneous impression with good-humored inflexibility then most when the whole cry of voices is on the other side. Else tomorrow a stranger will say with masterly good sense precisely what we have thought and felt all the time, and we shall be forced to take with shame our own opinion from another.

One would think from the talk of men that riches and poverty were a great matter; and our civilization mainly respects it. But the Indians say that they do not think the white man, with his brow of care, always toiling, afraid of heat and cold, and keeping within doors, has any advantage of them.

The permanent interest of every man is never to be in a false position, but to have the weight of nature to back him in all that he does. Riches and poverty are a thick or thin costume; and our life—the life of all of us—identical. For we transcend the circumstance continually and taste the real quality of existence; as in our employments, which only differ in the manifestations but express the same laws; or in our thoughts, which wear no silks and taste no ice-creams.

I prefer a tendency to stateliness to an excess of fellowship. Let the incommunicable objects of nature and the metaphysical isolation of man teach us independence. Let us not be too much acquainted. I would have a man enter his house through a hall filled with heroic and sacred sculptures, that he might not want the hint of tranquillity and self-poise. We should meet each morning as from foreign countries, and, spending the day together, should depart at night, as into foreign countries.

In all things I would have the island of a man inviolate. Let us sit apart as the gods, talking from peak to peak all round Olympus. No degree of affection need invade this religion. This is myrrh and rosemary to keep the other sweet. Lovers should guard their strangeness. If they forgive too much, all slides into confusion and meanness. It is easy to push this deference to a Chinese etiquette; but coolness and absence of heat and haste indicate fine qualities. A gentleman makes no noise; a lady is serene.

Proportionate is our disgust at those invaders who fill a studious house with blast and running, to secure some paltry convenience. Not less I dislike a low sympathy of each with his neighbor's needs. Must we have a good understanding with one another's palates? as foolish people who have lived long together know when each wants salt or sugar. I pray my companion, if he wishes for bread, to ask me for bread, and if he wishes for sassafras or arsenic, to ask me for them, and not to hold out his plate as if I knew already. Every natural function can be dignified by deliberation and privacy. Let us leave hurry to slaves. The compliments and ceremonies of our breeding should recall, however remotely, the grandeur of our destiny.

There is a time in every man's education when he arrives at the conviction that envy is ignorance; that imitation is suicide; that he must take himself for better or worse as his portion; that though the wide universe is full of good, no kernel of nourishing corn can come to him but through his toil bestowed on that plot of ground which is given to him to till. The power which resides in him is new in nature, and none but he knows what that is which he can do, nor does he know until he has tried.

I believe that our own experience instructs us that the secret of Education lies in respecting the pupil. It is not for you to choose what he shall know, what he shall do. It is chosen and foreordained, and he only holds the key to his own

secret. By your tampering and thwarting and too
much governing he may be hindered from his
end and kept out of his own. Respect the child.
Wait and see the new product of Nature. Nature
loves analogies, but not repetitions. Respect the
child. Be not too much his parent. Trespass not
on his solitude.

Whoso would be a man, must be a nonconform-
ist. He who would gather mortal palms must not
be hindered by the name of goodness, but must
explore if it be goodness. Nothing is at last sacred
but the integrity of your own mind.

Manners impress as they indicate real power. A
man who is sure of his point, carries a broad and
contented expression, which everybody reads.
And you cannot rightly train one to an air and
manner, except by making him the kind of man
of whom that manner is the natural expression.
Nature forever puts a premium on reality. What
is done for effect is seen to be done for effect;
what is done for love is felt to be done for love.

A man inspires affection and honor because he
was not lying in wait for these. The things of a
man for which we visit him were done in the
dark and cold. A little integrity is better than any
career. So deep are the sources of this surface-

action that even the size of your companion seems to vary with his freedom of thought. Not only is he larger, when at ease and his thoughts generous, but everything around him becomes variable with expression.

Let Nature bear the expense. The attitude, the tone, is all. Let our eyes not look away, but meet. Let us not look east and west for materials of conversation, but rest in presence and unity. A just feeling will fast enough supply fuel for discourse, if speaking be more grateful than silence. When people come to see us, we foolishly prattle, lest we be inhospitable. But things said for conversation are chalk eggs. Don't *say* things. What you *are* stands over you the while, and thunders so that I cannot hear what you say to the contrary. A lady of my acquaintance said, "I don't care so much for what they say as I do for what makes them say it."

These are ascending stairs—a good voice, winning manners, plain speech, chastened, however, by the schools into correctness; but we must come to the main matter, of power of statement —knowing your fact; hug your fact. For the essential thing is heat, and heat comes of sincerity. Speak what you do know and believe;

and are personally in it; and are answerable for every word. Eloquence is the power to translate a truth into language perfectly intelligible to the person to whom you speak.

In different hours a man represents each of several of his ancestors, as if there were seven or eight of us rolled up in each man's skin—seven or eight ancestors at least, and they constitute the variety of notes for that new piece of music which his life is. At the corner of the street you read the possibility of each passenger in the facial angle, in the complexion, in the depth of his eye. His parentage determines it.

Men are what their mothers made them. You may as well ask a loom which weaves huckabuck why it does not make cashmere, as expect poetry from this engineer, or a chemical discovery from that jobber. Ask the digger in the ditch to explain Newton's laws; the fine organs of his brain have been pinched by overwork and squalid poverty from father to son for a hundred years. When each comes forth from his mother's womb, the gate of gifts closes behind him.

I can do that by another which I cannot do alone. I can say to you what I cannot first say to myself. Other men are lenses through which we read our own minds. Each man seeks those of different quality from his own, and such as are good of their kind; that is, he seeks other men, and the *otherest*. The stronger the nature, the more it is reactive.

Accuracy is essential to beauty. The very definition of the intellect is Aristotle's: "that by which we know terms or boundaries." Give a boy accurate perceptions. Teach him the difference between the similar and the same. Make him call things by their right names. Pardon in him no blunder. Then he will give you solid satisfaction as long as he lives.

Life only avails, not the having lived. Power ceases in the instant of repose; it resides in the moment of transition from a past to a new state, in the shooting of the gulf, in the darting to an aim. This one fact the world hates; that the soul *becomes;* for that forever degrades the past, turns all riches to poverty, all reputation to a shame, confounds the saint with the rogue, shoves Jesus and Judas equally aside.

Each man has his own vocation. The talent is the call. There is one direction in which all space is open to him. He has faculties silently inviting him thither to endless exertion. He is like a ship in a river; he runs against obstructions on every side but one, on that side all obstruction is taken away and he sweeps serenely over a deepening channel into an infinite sea. This talent and this call depend on his organization, or the mode in which the general soul incarnates itself in him. He inclines to do something which is easy to him and good when it is done, but which no other man can do. He has no rival. For the more truly he consults his own powers, the more difference will his work exhibit from the work of any other.

A man passes for that he is worth. Very idle is all curiosity concerning other people's estimate of us, and all fear of remaining unknown is not less so. If a man know that he can do any thing, —that he can do it better than any one else,—he has a pledge of the acknowledgment of that fact by all persons. The world is full of judgment days, and into every assembly that a man enters, in every action he attempts, he is gauged and stamped.

He has seen but half the universe who never has been shown the house of Pain. As the salt sea covers more than two thirds of the surface of

the globe, so sorrow encroaches in man on felic-
ity. The conversation of men is a mixture of
regrets and apprehensions. I do not know but
the prevalent hue of things to the eye of leisure
is melancholy. In the dark hours, our existence
seems to be a defensive war, a struggle against
the encroaching All, which threatens surely to
engulf soon, and is impatient of our short
reprieve.

We remember those things which we love and
those things which we hate. The memory of all
men is robust on the subject of a debt due to
them, or of an insult inflicted on them. "They
can remember," as [Dr.] Johnson said, "who
kicked them last."

What would it avail me, if I could destroy my
enemies? There would be as many tomorrow.
That which I hate and fear is really in myself,
and no knife is long enough to reach to its heart.

If you would not be known to do any thing,
never do it. A man may play the fool in the drifts
of a desert, but every grain of sand shall seem
to see. He may be a solitary eater, but he cannot
keep his foolish counsel. A broken complexion, a
swinish look, ungenerous acts and the want of

due knowledge,—all blab. Can a cook, a Chif-
finch, an Iachimo be mistaken for Zeno or Paul?
Confucius exclaimed,—"How can a man be concealed? How can a man be concealed?"

The perception of the Comic is a tie of sympathy
with other men, a pledge of sanity, and a pro-
tection from those perverse tendencies and
gloomy insanities in which fine intellects sometimes lose themselves. A rogue alive to the ludi-
crous is still convertible. If that sense is lost, his
fellow men can do little for him.

If you visit your friend, why need you apologize
for not having visited him, and waste his time
and deface your own act? Visit him now. Let
him feel that the highest love has come to see
him, in thee its lowest organ. Or why need you
torment yourself and friend by secret self-re-
proaches that you have not assisted him or com-
plimented him with gifts and salutations here-
tofore? Be a gift and a benediction. Shine with
real light and not with the borrowed reflection
of gifts.

Each man sees his own life defaced and disfig-
ured, as the life of man is not to his imagination.
Each man sees over his own experience a certain

stain of error, whilst that of other men looks fair and ideal. . . . Every thing is beautiful seen from the point of the intellect, or as truth. But all is sour if seen as experience. Details are melancholy; the plan is seemly and noble.

We have a great deal more kindness than is ever spoken. Maugre all the selfishness that chills like east winds the world, the whole human family is bathed with an element of love like a fine ether. How many persons we meet in houses, whom we scarcely speak to, whom yet we honor, and who honor us! How many we see in the street, or sit with in church, whom, though silently, we warmly rejoice to be with! Read the language of these wandering eye-beams. The heart knoweth.

I awoke this morning with devout thanksgiving for my friends, the old and the new. Shall I not call God the Beautiful, who daily showeth himself so to me in his gifts? I chide society, I embrace solitude, and yet I am not so ungrateful as not to see the wise, the lovely and the noble-minded, as from time to time they pass my gate. Who hears me, who understands me, becomes mine,—a possession for all time.

Nor is Nature so poor but she gives me this

joy several times, and thus we weave social threads of our own, a new web of relations; and, as many thoughts in succession substantiate themselves, we shall by and by stand in a new world of our own creation, and no longer strangers and pilgrims in a traditionary globe. My friends have come to me unsought. The great God gave them to me. By oldest right, by the divine affinity of virtue with itself, I find them, or rather not I but the Deity in me and in them derides and cancels the thick walls of individual character, relation, age, sex, circumstance, at which he usually connives, and now makes many one.

It is not the office of a man to receive gifts. How dare you give them? We wish to be self-sustained. We do not quite forgive a giver. The hand that feeds us is in some danger of being bitten. We can receive anything from love, for that is a way of receiving it from ourselves; but not from anyone who assumes to bestow. We sometimes hate the meat which we eat, because there seems something of degrading dependence in living by it.

What is so great as friendship, let us carry with what grandeur of spirit we can. Let us be silent,

—so we may hear the whisper of the gods. Let us not interfere. Who set you to cast about what you should say to the select souls, or how to say anything to such? No matter how ingenious, no matter how graceful and bland. There are innumerable degrees of folly and wisdom, and for you to say aught is to be frivolous. Wait, and thy heart shall speak. Wait until the necessary and everlasting overpowers you, until day and night avail themselves of your lips. The only reward of virtue is virtue; the only way to have a friend is to be one.

The key to every man is his thought. Sturdy and defying though he look, he has a helm which he obeys, which is the idea after which all his facts are classified. He can only be reformed by showing him a new idea which commands his own. The life of man is a self-evolving circle, which, from a ring imperceptibly small, rushes on all sides outwards to new and larger circles, and that without end. The extent to which this generation of circles, wheel without wheel, will go, depends on the force or truth of the individual soul.

Books are the best of things, well used; abused, among the worst. What is the right use? What is the one end which all means go to effect? They are for nothing but to inspire. I had better never see a book than to be warped by its attraction clean out of my own orbit, and made a satellite instead of a system.

The one thing in the world, of value, is the active soul. This every man is entitled to; this every man contains within him, although in almost all men obstructed and as yet unborn. The soul active sees absolute truth and utters truth, or creates. In this action it is genius; not the privilege of here and there a favorite, but the sound estate of every man.

The book, the college, the school of art, the institution of any kind, stop with some past utterance of genius. This is good, say they—let us hold by this. They pin me down. They look backward and not forward. But genius looks forward: the eyes of man are set in his forehead, not in his hindhead: man hopes: genius creates. Whatever talents may be, if the man create not, the pure efflux of the Deity is not his—cinders and smoke there may be, but not yet flame. There are creative manners, there are creative actions, and creative words; manners, actions, words, that is, indicative of no custom or authority, but springing spontaneous from the mind's own sense of good and fair.

On the Greatness of Men

Emerson's constructive view of man's energies and possibilities compelled him to envision the true extent of greatness among men, searching how it comes about that some men are considered great, and how their greatness alters history. "An institution is the lengthened shadow of one man." As an American patriot, Emerson was tasking himself to find an outline for heroism that would shape the teeming new nation that swelled before him. Europe had her heroes; America must also have hers, silhouetted before different lights, grown tall on different soil.

Great men serve us as insurrections do in bad governments. The world would run into endless routine, and forms incrust forms, till the life was gone. But the perpetual supply of new genius shocks us with thrills of life, and recalls us to principles.

Miracle comes to the miraculous, not to the arithmetician. Talent and success interest me but moderately. The great class, they who affect our imagination, the men who could not make their hands meet around their objects, the rapt, the lost, the fools of ideas—they suggest what they cannot execute. They speak to the ages, and are heard from afar.

Difficulties exist to be surmounted. The great heart will no more complain of the obstructions that make success hard, than of the iron walls of the gun which hinder the shot from scattering. It was walled round with iron tube with that purpose, to give it irresistible force in one direction. A strenuous soul hates cheap successes. It is the ardor of the assailant that makes the vigor of the defender. The great are not tender at being obscure, despised, insulted. Such only feel themselves in adverse fortune. Strong men greet war, tempest, hard times, which search till they find resistance and bottom. They wish, as Pindar said, "to tread the floors of hell, with necessities as hard as iron."

A foolish consistency is the hobgoblin of little minds, adored by little statesmen and philosophers and divines. With consistency a great soul has simply nothing to do. He may as well concern himself with his shadow on the wall. Speak what you think now in hard words and tomorrow speak what tomorrow thinks in hard words again, though it contradict everything you said today.—"Ah, so you shall be sure to be misunderstood."—Is it so bad then to be misunderstood? Pythagoras was misunderstood, and Socrates, and Jesus, and Luther, and Copernicus, and Galileo, and Newton, and every pure and wise spirit that ever took flesh. To be great is to be misunderstood.

Life is a scale of degrees. Between rank and rank of our great men are wide intervals. Mankind have in all ages attached themselves to a few persons who either by the quality of that idea they embodied or by the largeness of their reception were entitled to the positions of leaders and law-givers. These teach us the qualities of primary nature—admit us to the constitution of things. We swim, day by day, on a river of delusions and are effectually amused with houses and towns in the air, of which the men about us are dupes.

But life is a sincerity. In lucid intervals we say, "Let there be an entrance opened for me into realities; I have worn the fool's cap too long." We will know the meaning of our economies and politics. Give us the cipher, and if persons and things are scores of a celestial music, let us read off the strains. We have been cheated of our reason; yet there have been sane men, who enjoyed a rich and related existence. What they know, they know for us. With each new mind, a new secret of nature transpires; nor can the Bible be closed until the last great man is born.

There are not in the world at any one time more than a dozen persons who read and understand Plato,—never enough to pay for an edition of his works; yet to every generation these come duly down, for the sake of those few persons, as if God brought them in his hand.

No object really interests us but man, and in man only his superiorities; and though we are aware of a perfect law in nature, it has fascination for us only through its relation to him, or as it is rooted in the mind.

Nature makes fifty poor melons for one that is good, and shakes down a tree full of gnarled, wormy, unripe crabs, before you can find a dozen dessert apples; and she scatters nations of naked Indians and nations of clothed Christians, with two or three good heads among them. Nature works very hard, and only hits the white

once in a million throws. In mankind she is contented if she yields one master in a century. The
more difficulty there is in creating good men,
the more they are used when they come.

. . . The effect of every action is measured by
the depth of the sentiment from which it pro-
ceeds. The great man knew not that he was
great. It took a century or two for that fact to
appear. What he did, he did because he must; it
was the most natural thing in the world, and
grew out of the circumstances of the moment.
But now, every thing he did, even to the lifting
of his finger or the eating of bread, looks large,
all-related, and is called an institution.

These are the demonstrations in a few par-
ticulars of the genius of nature; they show the
direction of the stream. But the stream is blood;
every drop is alive.

Trust thyself: every heart vibrates to that iron
string. Accept the place the divine providence
has found for you, the society of your contem-
poraries, the connection of events. Great men
have always done so, and confided themselves
childlike to the genius of their age, betraying
their perception that the absolutely truthworthy
was seated at their heart, working through their

hands, predominating in all their being. And we are now men, and must accept in the highest mind the same transcendent destiny; and not minors and invalids in a protected corner, not cowards fleeting before a revolution, but guides, redeemers and benefactors, obeying the Almighty effort and advancing on Chaos and the Dark.

We consecrate a great deal of nonsense because it was allowed by great men. There is none without his foible. I believe that if an angel should come to chant the chorus of the moral law, he would eat too much gingerbread, or take liberties with private letters, or do some precious atrocity.

On America

*America, for Emerson, was the wave of the
future. It follows that in his best and
worst of times, when corrupt government,
slavery, and civil war almost capsized
American democracy, he would be enraged
at the distance between reality and dream.
Thus he found cause to love his ideal
of America while hating the political life of
the real America he inhabited. Here he
swings between the magnetic poles of
those feelings.*

. . . We only say, Let us live in America, too
thankful for our want of feudal institutions. Our
houses and towns are like mosses and lichens, so
slight and new; but youth is a fault of which
we shall daily mend. This land too is as old as
the Flood, and wants no ornament or privilege
which nature could bestow. Here stars, here
woods, here hills, here animals, here men
abound, and the vast tendencies concur of a new
order. If only the men are employed in conspir-
ing with the designs of the Spirit who led us
hither and is leading us still, we shall quickly
enough advance out of all hearing of others' cen-

sures, out of all regrets of our own, into a new
and more excellent social state than history has
recorded.

The apple is our national fruit. In October, the
country is covered with its ornamental harvests.
The American sun paints itself in these glowing
balls amid the green leaves, the social fruit, in
which Nature has deposited every possible fla-
vor; whole zones and climates she has concen-
trated into apples.

I am afraid you do not understand values.
Look over the fence at the farmer who stands
there. He makes every cloud in the sky, and
every beam of the sun, serve him. His trees are
full of brandy. He saves every drop of sap, as if
it were wine. A few years ago those trees were
whipsticks. Now, every one of them is worth a
hundred dollars. Observe their form; not a
branch nor a twig is to spare. They look as if
they were arms and fingers, holding out to you
balls of fire and gold. One tree yields the rent of
an acre of land.

There is no event but sprung somewhere from
the soul of man; and therefore there is none but
the soul of man can interpret. Every presenti-
ment of the mind is executed somewhere in a

gigantic fact. What else is Greece, Rome, England, France, St. Helena? What else are churches, literatures, and empires? The new man must feel that he is new, and has not come into the world mortgaged to the opinions and usages of Europe, and Asia, and Egypt.

The sense of spiritual independence is like the lovely varnish of the dew, whereby the old, hard, peaked earth and its old self-same productions are made new every morning, and shining with the last touch of the artist's hand. A false humility, a complaisance to reigning schools or to the wisdom of antiquity, must not defraud me of supreme possession of this hour. If any person have less love of liberty and less jealousy to guard his integrity, shall he therefore dictate to you and me? . . . Now that we are here we will put our own interpretation on things, and our own things for interpretation.

All our political disasters grow as logically out of our attempts in the past to do without justice, as the sinking of some part of your house comes of defect in the foundation. One thing is plain; a certain personal virtue is essential to freedom; and it begins to be doubtful whether our corruption in this country has not gone a little over the mark of safety, so that when canvassed we shall be found to be made up of a majority of reckless self-seekers. The divine knowledge has ebbed out of us and we do not know enough to be free.

We have yet had no genius in America, with tyrannous eye, which knew the value of our incomparable materials, and saw, in the barbarism and materialism of the times, another carnival of the same gods whose picture he so much admires in Homer; then in the Middle Age; then in Calvinism. Banks and tariffs, the newspaper and caucus, Methodism and Unitarianism, are flat and dull to dull people, but rest on the same foundations of wonder as the town of Troy and the temple of Delphi, and are as swiftly passing away. Our log-rolling, our stumps and their politics, our fisheries, our Negroes and Indians, our boats and our repudiations, the wrath of rogues and the pusillanimity of honest men, the northern trade, the southern planting, the western clearing, Oregon and Texas, are yet unsung. Yet America is a poem in our eyes; its ample geography dazzles the imagination, and it will not wait long for metres.

In America the geography is sublime, but the men are not: the inventions are excellent, but the inventors one is sometimes ashamed of. The agencies by which events so grand as the opening of California, of Texas, of Oregon, and the junction of the two oceans, are effected, are paltry — coarse selfishness, fraud and conspiracy; and most of the great results of history are brought about by discreditable means.

Concord Hymn

By the rude bridge that arched the flood,
Their flag to April's breeze unfurled,
Here once the embattled farmers stood,
And fired the shot heard round the world.

The foe long since in silence slept;
Alike the conqueror silent sleeps;
And Time the ruined bridge has swept
Down the dark stream which seaward creeps.

On this green bank, by this soft stream,
We set today a votive stone;
That memory may their deed redeem,
When, like our sires, our sons are gone.

Spirit, that made those spirits dare
To die, and leave their children free,
Bid Time and Nature gently spare
The shaft we raise to them and thee.

There, I thought, in America, lies nature sleeping, overgrowing, almost conscious, too much by half for man in the picture, and so giving a certain *tristesse*, like the rank vegetation of swamps and forests seen at night, steeped in dews and rains, which it loves; and on it man seems not able to make much impression. There, in that great sloven continent, in high Allegheny pastures, in the sea-wide sky-skirted prairie, still sleeps and murmurs and hides the great mother. . . .

Let us honestly state the facts. Our America has a bad name for superficialness. Great men, great nations, have not been boasters and buffoons, but perceivers of the terror of life, and have manned themselves to face it.

The spirit of our American radicalism is destructive and aimless: it is not loving; it has no ulterior and divine ends, but is destructive only out of hatred and selfishness. On the other side, the conservative party, composed of the most moderate, able and cultivated part of the population, is timid, and merely defensive of property. It vindicates no right, it aspires to no real good, it brands no crime, it proposes no generous policy; it does not build, nor write, nor cherish the arts, nor foster religion, nor establish schools, nor encourage science, nor emancipate the slave, nor befriend the poor, or the Indian, or the immigrant. From neither party, when in power, has the world any benefit to expect in science, art, or humanity, at all commensurate with the resources of the nation.

You who quarrel with the arrangements of society, and are willing to embroil all, and risk the indisputable good that exists, for the chance of better, live, move, and have your being in this, and your deeds contradict your words every day. For as you cannot jump from the ground without using the resistance of the ground, nor put out the boat to sea without shoving from the shore, nor attain liberty without rejecting obligation, so you are under the necessity of using the actual order of things, in order to disuse it; to live by it, whilst you wish to take away its life.

The past has baked your loaf, and in the strength of its bread you would break up the oven. But you are betrayed by your own nature. You also are conservatives. However men please to style themselves, I see no other than a conservative party. You are not only identical with us in your needs, but also in your methods and aims. You quarrel with my conservatism, but it is to build up one of your own; it will have a new beginning, but the same course and end, the same trials, the same passions; among the lovers of the new I observe that there is a jealousy of the newest, and that the seceder from the seceder is as damnable as the pope himself. . . .

Every actual State is corrupt. Good men must not obey the laws too well. What satire on government can equal the severity of censure conveyed in the word *politic*, which now for ages has signified *cunning*, intimating that the State is a trick?

Emerson's Wit

Wit was second nature to Emerson—not only humor, which at his hands was dry, canny, masterly—but wit in the old sense of finding connections in seemingly disconnected things. His pithy epigrams, nuts and nuggets of thought, brought home to the audiences to whom he lectured the heart of his ideas, and lodged themselves in his hearers' memories. Many of his sayings have joined the language as proverbs. Some of the most famous are collected here.

Heaven always bears some proportion to earth.

Beauty without grace
                     is the hook without the bait.

You can no more keep out of politics than you can keep out of the frost.

Our chief want in life is somebody who shall make us do what we can.

I like dry light, and hard clouds, hard expressions, and hard manners.

If an American should wake up some morning and discover that his existence was unnecessary, he would think himself excessively ill-used, and would declare himself instantly against the government of the Universe.

We must be as courteous to a man as we are to a picture, which we are willing to give the advantage of a good light.

Shallow men believe in luck.

Nationality is often silly. Every nation believes that the Divine Providence has a sneaking kindness for it.

All the thoughts of a turtle are turtle.

Great men are they who see that spiritual is stronger than any material force; that thoughts rule the world.

This shining moment is an edifice
Which the Omnipotent cannot rebuild.

I suppose you could never prove to the mind of the most ingenious mollusk that such a creature as a whale was possible.

A man is a bundle of relations, a knot of roots,
whose flower and fruitage is the world.

The great always introduce us to facts;
　　　small men introduce us always to themselves.

We do not count a man's years until he has nothing left to count.

The loves of flint and iron
　　　　　are naturally a little rougher
　　　　　than those of the nightingale and the rose.

Of all wit's uses the main one
Is to live well with who has none.

Life consists in what a man is thinking of all day.

I like the sayers of No better
　　　　　　　　than the sayers of Yes.

The ornament of a house
　　　　　　is the friends who frequent it.

Hitch your wagon to a star.

'Tis bad when believers and unbelievers live in
the same manner—I distrust the religion.

Bores are good too. They may help you to a good indignation, if not to a sympathy.

To live without duties is obscene.

Great geniuses have the shortest biographies.

Solitude, the safeguard of mediocrity,
is to genius the stern friend.

Next to the originator of a good sentence is the first quoter of it.

God works in moments.

Wit makes its own welcome,
and levels all distinctions.

There are some men above grief
and some men below it.

Nothing is old but the mind.

An institution is the lengthened shadow of one man.

A friend may well be reckoned the masterpiece of Nature.

Do what we can, summer will have its flies. If we walk in the woods, we must feed the mosquitos.

The only reward of virtue is virtue; the only way to have a friend is to be one.

Every sweet has its sour; every evil its good.

I do then with my friends as I do with my books. I would have them where I can find them, but I seldom use them.

For every thing you have missed, you have gained something else; and for every thing you gain, you lose something.

Nothing can bring you peace but yourself.

Criticism should not be querulous and wasting, all knife and root-puller, but guiding, instructive, inspiring, a south wind, not an east wind.

The true test of civilization is, not the census, or the size of cities, nor the crops—no, but the kind of man the country turns out.

A friend is a person with whom I may be sincere. Before him, I may think aloud.

I have no right of nomination in the choice of my friends. Sir, I should be happy to oblige you, but my friends must elect themselves.

There is always a best way of doing everything, if it be to boil an egg. Manners are the happy ways of doing things.

Everything in Nature contains all the powers of Nature. Everything is made of one hidden stuff.

In skating over thin ice our safety is our speed.

All mankind love a lover.

Heroism feels and never reasons and therefore is always right.

Happy is the house that shelters a friend.

Nothing great
            was ever achieved without enthusiasm.

Nature and Books
            belong to the eyes that see them.

He is great who is what he is from Nature, and who never reminds us of others.

Nothing astonishes men so much as common sense and plain dealing.

The reward of a thing well done,
                    is to have done it.

The only gift is a portion of thyself.

Important Dates in
Emerson's Life

1803 Born in Boston, Mass., May 25.

1821 Graduated from Harvard College.

1825 After a period of school teaching,
      entered Cambridge Divinity School.

1826 Ordained a Unitarian minister; fell ill;
      went south for recuperation.

1827 Returned to Boston; married Ellen
      Tucker of Concord, Mass.; appointed
      minister of Second Church (Unitarian)

1832 Wife, Ellen, died; left Second Church;
      toured Europe; met Coleridge, Carlyle,
      Wordsworth, and other English writers.

1833 Returned to Boston; began lecture career.

1835 Married Lydia Jackson of Plymouth, Mass.

1837 Phi Beta Kappa oration at Harvard,
      "The American Scholar."

1841-44 *Essays* published in two volumes.

1856 Impressions of England published in
      English Traits.

1872 House burns down; rebuilt by popular
      subscription.

1882 Died April 27; buried at Sleepy Hollow,
      Concord, Mass.

Set at The Castle Press in Intertype Walbaum,
a light, open typeface designed by
Justus Erich Walbaum (1768-1839),
who was a type founder at Weimar.
Printed on Hallmark Eggshell Book paper.
Designed by Harald Peter.